W9-BCB-594

# CHRISTMAS
## *Patchwork Loves Embroidery*

*Hand Stitches, Holiday Projects*

### *Gail Pan*

Martingale®
Create with Confidence

Christmas Patchwork Loves Embroidery:
Hand Stitches, Holiday Projects
© 2016 by Gail Pan

Martingale®
19021 120th Ave. NE, Ste. 102
Bothell, WA 98011-9511 USA
ShopMartingale.com

Printed in China
21 20 19 18 17 16          8 7 6 5 4 3 2 1

Library of Congress Cataloging-in-Publication Data
is available upon request.

ISBN: 978-1-60468-693-7

## MISSION STATEMENT

We empower makers who use fabric and yarn
to make life more enjoyable.

## CREDITS

PUBLISHER AND
CHIEF VISIONARY OFFICER
Jennifer Erbe Keltner

CONTENT DIRECTOR
Karen Costello Soltys

DESIGN MANAGER
Adrienne Smitke

MANAGING EDITOR
Tina Cook

PRODUCTION MANAGER
Regina Girard

ACQUISITIONS EDITOR
Karen M. Burns

PHOTOGRAPHER
Brent Kane

TECHNICAL EDITOR
Nancy Mahoney

ILLUSTRATOR
Christine Erikson

COPY EDITOR
Marcy Heffernan

# CONTENTS

keep Christmas in
your heart ♥♥ and
home, all year long

# INTRODUCTION

*The projects in this book are designed to celebrate Christmas and enable you to decorate your home or make a gift for family and friends. Don't be afraid to mix and match the designs. If you want to make a smaller quilt or change the design to be on a bag or table runner instead, then feel free! Please also feel confident in picking your own color schemes—it's your choice!*

*I hope you enjoy the projects in this book and find stitching for Christmas a lot of fun. Just like I do!*

*~ Gail*

# BIRDSONG TABLE QUILT

*Stitch a cute little quilt to adorn your table.*

*Birdsong Table Quilt*

FINISHED QUILT: 34½" x 34½" • FINISHED BLOCK: 8" x 8"

## Materials

*Yardage is based on 42"-wide fabric.*

⅞ yard of red print for Star blocks and outer border

⅝ yard of green dot for Star blocks, inner border, and binding

½ yard of cream print for Star blocks

⅓ yard of cream tone on tone for embroidery background

1⅛ yards of fabric for backing

38" x 38" piece of batting

⅝ yard of lightweight fusible interfacing, 18" to 20" wide, for embroidery backing

6-strand embroidery floss in dark green, light green, red, and yellow

Ecru pearl cotton, size 8

¼" quilter's tape (optional, see page 78)

## Cutting

**From the cream tone on tone, cut:**

4 squares, 9" x 9"

**From the lightweight fusible interfacing, cut:**

4 squares, 9" x 9"

**From the green dot, cut:**

5 strips, 2½" x 42"; crosscut *1 of the strips* into:
    4 squares, 2½" x 2½"
    4 rectangles, 2½" x 4½"

4 strips, 1½" x 42"; crosscut into:
    2 strips, 1½" x 24½"
    2 strips, 1½" x 26½"

**From the cream print, cut:**

1 strip, 4½" x 42"; crosscut into 5 squares, 4½" x 4½"

3 strips, 2½" x 42"; crosscut into 40 squares, 2½" x 2½"

**From the red print, cut:**

3 strips, 2½" x 42"; crosscut into:
    16 squares, 2½" x 2½"
    16 rectangles, 2½" x 4½"

4 strips, 4½" x 42"; crosscut into:
    2 strips, 4½" x 26½"
    2 strips, 4½" x 34½"

## Embroidering the Designs

1. Using the pattern on page 10, trace the Birdsong design onto the right side of each cream 9" square. Fuse a square of interfacing to the wrong side of each marked square.

2. Using two strands of floss, embroider the designs, following the embroidery key and color guides on the pattern.

3. Gently press the stitched squares. Centering the embroidered design and aligning the 45° line on your ruler with the tree trunk, trim the squares to 8½" x 8½". Set aside.

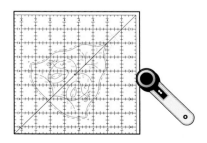

## Making the Blocks

1. Mark a diagonal line on the wrong side of eight cream-print 2½" squares. Aligning the corners, pin a marked square on one end of a green rectangle, right sides together. Sew directly on the marked line. Trim ¼" from the seamline and press the seam allowances as indicated. Repeat for the other corner to make a flying-geese unit. Make four units.

Make 4.

2. Lay out the flying-geese units from step 1, four green squares, and one cream-print 4½" square as shown above right. Sew the pieces together in rows. Press the seam allowances as indicated.

Sew the rows together to make one green Star block. Press the seam allowances toward the center.

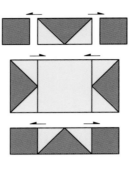

Make 1.

3. Repeat steps 1 and 2 to make four red Star blocks.

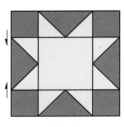

Make 4.

## Assembling the Quilt Top

1. Lay out the Star blocks and the embroidered squares in three rows as shown. Sew the blocks and squares together in rows. Press the seam allowances as indicated. Sew the rows together. Press the seam allowances away from the embroidered squares. The quilt top should measure 24½" x 24½".

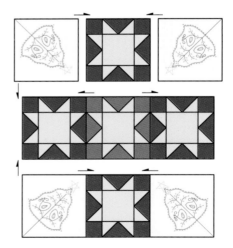

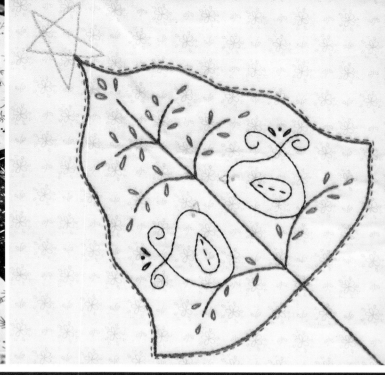

2. Sew the green 24½"-long strips to opposite sides of the quilt top. Press the seam allowances toward the green strips. Sew the green 26½"-long strips to the top and bottom of the quilt top. Press the seam allowances toward the green strips.

3. Sew the red 26½"-long strips to opposite sides of the quilt top. Press the seam allowances toward the red strips. Sew the red 34½"-long strips to the top and bottom of the quilt top. Press the seam allowances toward the red strips.

Quilt assembly

## Finishing the Quilt

1. Layer the quilt top, batting, and backing; baste. Using pearl cotton and big-stitch quilting (see page 78), quilt ¼" inside the squares and triangles in the Star blocks and ¼" from the seamline in the inner and outer borders.

### QUILTING TIP

*Attach the binding before quilting ¼" from the binding seam. That way the quilting line will be exactly ¼" from the seamline.*

2. Trim the batting and backing to the same size as the top.

3. Using the green 2½"-wide strips, make and attach the binding before completing the quilting next to the binding seam.

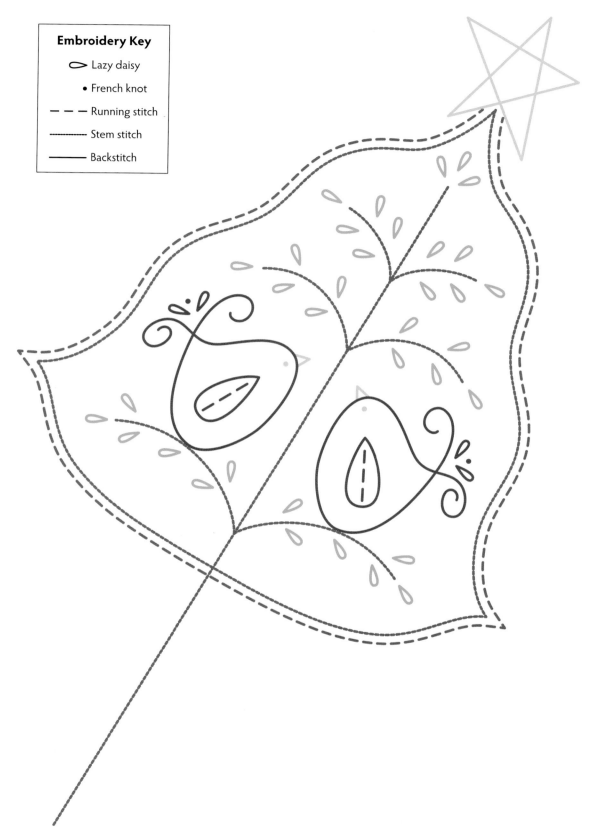

**Embroidery Key**

⬯ Lazy daisy

• French knot

– – – Running stitch

·········· Stem stitch

——— Backstitch

**Birdsong Table Quilt**

# CHRISTMAS BAUBLES WALL HANGING

*Nine stitched baubles adorn this large wall quilt.*

*Christmas Baubles Wall Hanging*

FINISHED SIZE: 42½" x 42½" • FINISHED BLOCK: 10" x 10"

## Materials

*Yardage is based on 42"-wide fabric.*

⅛ yard *each* of 9 assorted red prints for blocks and cornerstones

¾ yard of red floral for border

½ yard of cream-star fabric for embroidery background

½ yard of red-and-cream floral for sashing

½ yard of red-star print for binding

2¾ yards of fabric for backing

46" x 46" piece of batting

1 yard of lightweight fusible interfacing, 18" to 20" wide, for embroidery backing

Dark-red pearl cotton, size 12

Ecru pearl cotton, size 8

¼" quilter's tape (optional, see page 78)

## Cutting

**From the cream-star fabric, cut:**

2 strips, 7" x 42"; crosscut into 9 squares, 7" x 7"

**From the lightweight fusible interfacing, cut:**

9 squares, 7" x 7"

**From *each* of the assorted red prints, cut:***

2 strips, 1½" x 44"; crosscut into:
    2 strips, 1½" x 6½" (18 total)
    4 strips, 1½" x 8½" (36 total)
    2 strips, 1½" x 10½" (18 total)
    2 squares 1½" x 1½" (18 total, 2 will be extra)

**From the red-and-cream floral, cut;**

8 strips, 1½" x 42"; crosscut into 24 strips, 1½" x 10½"

**From the red floral, cut;**

4 strips, 4½" x 42"

**From the red-star print, cut;**

5 strips, 2½" x 42"

*Sort the strips into 9 matching sets of 2 strips, each 1½" x 6½", and 2 strips, each 1½" x 8½". You'll also need 9 matching sets of 2 strips, each 1½" x 8½", and 2 strips, each 1½" x 10½".*

## Embroidering the Designs

1. Using the patterns on pages 15–19, trace a different Christmas Baubles design onto the right side of each cream square. Fuse a square of interfacing to the wrong side of each marked square.

2. Using one strand of dark-red pearl cotton, embroider the designs following the embroidery key on the pattern. Freehand embroider a running stitch inside each bauble (not marked on the design).

### FEWER TANGLES

*Using shorter lengths of floss will make for fewer knots. Threading the needle more often is easier than having to frequently stop and untangle knots.*

## Making the Blocks

Each block uses two sets of four matching red strips: the first set is comprised of two strips that are 1½" x 6½" and two that are 1½" x 8½". The second set has two strips that are 1½" x 8½" and two that are 1½" x 10½".

1. Centering the embroidered design, trim the stitched squares to 6½" x 6½".

2. Sew red 1½" x 6½" strips to opposite sides of an embroidered square. Press the seam allowances toward the red strips. Sew red 1½" x 8½" strips to the top and bottom of the embroidered square. Press the seam allowances toward the red strips.

3. Repeat step 2, sewing matching 1½" x 8½" and 1½" x 10½" strips to the unit from step 2 to make a block. Make nine blocks.

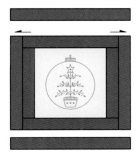

Make 9.

## Assembling the Wall-Hanging Top

1. Join four red squares and three red-and-cream floral strips, alternating them as shown to make a sashing row. Press the seam allowances as indicated. Make a total of four rows.

Make 4.

2. Join four red-and-cream strips and three embroidered blocks to make a block row. Press the seam allowances as indicated. Make a total of three rows.

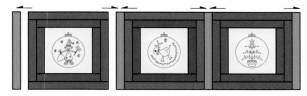

Make 3.

3. Sew the sashing and block rows together, alternating them as shown in the quilt assembly diagram on page 14. Press the seam allowances toward the sashing rows.

4. Sew the red-floral strips together end to end. From the pieced strip, cut two 34½"-long strips and two 42½"-long strips. Sew the 34½"-long strips to opposite sides of the quilt top. Press the seam allowances toward the border. Sew the

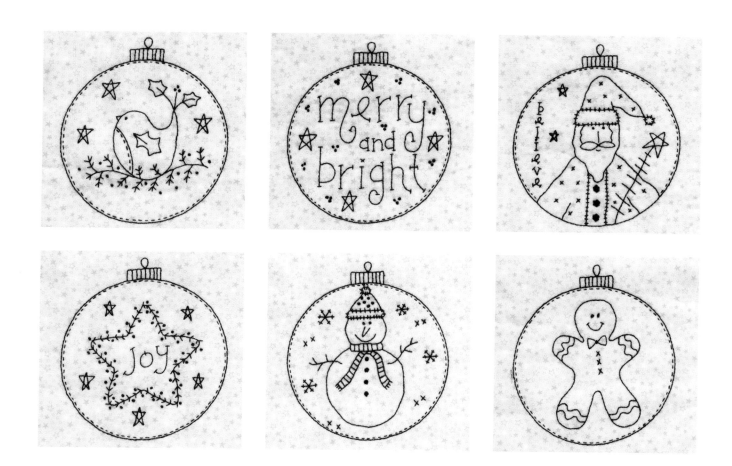

42½"-long strips to the top and bottom of the quilt top. Press the seam allowances toward the border.

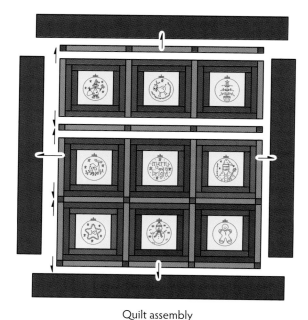

Quilt assembly

## Finishing the Wall Hanging

1. Layer the wall-hanging top, batting, and backing; baste. Using ecru pearl cotton and big-stitch quilting (see page 78), quilt ¼" inside each embroidered square, a wavy line in the center of each red strip, ¼" from each seamline in the border, and a wavy line in the center of the border.

2. Trim the batting and backing to the same size as the top.

3. To make an optional hanging sleeve prior to binding, fold under the ends of a 5" x 38" strip by ¼" twice and topstitch to hem. Fold the strip in half lengthwise, *wrong* sides together, and press. Aligning the raw edges, stitch the folded strip to the top of the quilt back, ⅛" from the raw edges.

4. Using the red-star 2½"-wide strips, make and attach the binding *before* completing the quilting next to the binding seam (do not quilt through the sleeve if there is one). Stitch the lower (folded) edge of the sleeve to the backing by hand.

## Embroidery Key

◠ Lazy daisy

• French knot

✕✕ Cross-stitch

— Backstitch

**Christmas Baubles Wall Hanging**

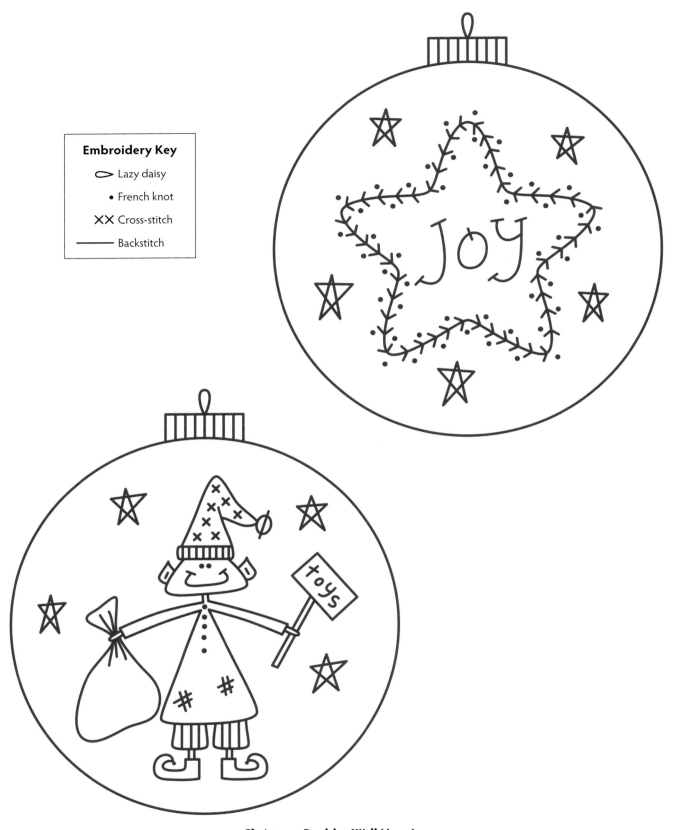

**Embroidery Key**

- Lazy daisy
- French knot
- Cross-stitch
- Backstitch

JOY

toys

**Christmas Baubles Wall Hanging**

*christmas patchwork loves embroidery*

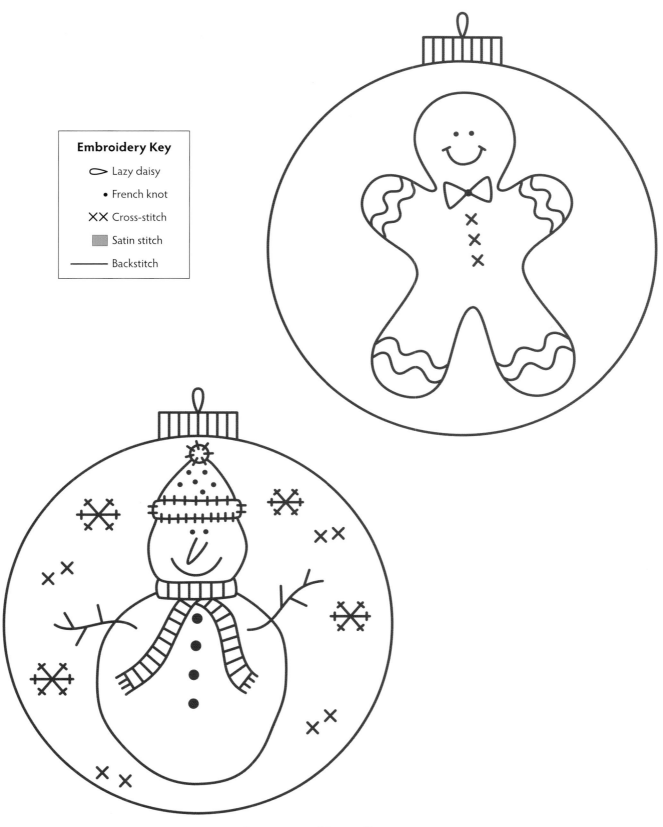

**Embroidery Key**

- ⌒ Lazy daisy
- • French knot
- ✕✕ Cross-stitch
- ▨ Satin stitch
- — Backstitch

**Christmas Baubles Wall Hanging**

**Embroidery Key**

- Lazy daisy
- French knot
- Cross-stitch
- Satin stitch
- Backstitch

believe

merry and bright

**Christmas Baubles Wall Hanging**

**Embroidery Key**

- Lazy daisy
- French knot
- Cross-stitch
- Running stitch
- Satin stitch
- Backstitch

**Christmas Baubles Wall Hanging**

# JOY TO THE WORLD PILLOW

*A redwork pillow is just right for Christmas decorating.*

*Joy to the World Pillow*

• FINISHED SIZE: 16" x 16" •

## Materials

*Yardage is based on 42"-wide fabric.*

½ yard *total* of assorted red prints for pillow front

1 rectangle, 10" x 12", of cream fabric for embroidery background

¼ yard of red print for binding

1 fat quarter (18" x 21") of fabric for pillow backing

18" x 18" piece of batting

1 rectangle, 10" x 12", of lightweight fusible interfacing for embroidery backing

6-strand embroidery floss in variegated red

Ecru pearl cotton, size 8

16" x 16" pillow form

¼" quilter's tape (optional, see page 78)

## Cutting

**From the assorted red prints, cut:**

1 strip, 1½" x 8½" (A)

1 strip, 2½" x 11½" (B)

1 strip, 1½" x 10½" (C)

2 strips, 2½" x 12½" (D and E)

2 strips, 2½" x 14½" (F and G)

1 strip, 2½" x 16½" (H)

**From the backing fabric, cut:**

2 rectangles, 8½" x 16½"

**From the red print for binding, cut:**

2 strips, 2½" x 42"

## Embroidering the Designs

1. Using the pattern on page 23, trace the Joy to the World design onto the right side of the cream rectangle. Fuse the rectangle of interfacing to the wrong side of the marked rectangle.

2. Using two strands of floss, stitch the design, following the embroidery key on the pattern.

## Making the Pillow Top

Refer to the diagram following step 5 on page 22 for placement guidance throughout. After sewing each seam, press the seam allowances toward the newly added strip.

1. Centering the design, trim the embroidered rectangle to 8½" x 10½". Sew the red A strip to the bottom of the embroidered rectangle.

2. Sew the red B strip to the right side of the stitched rectangle. Sew the red C strip to the top of the rectangle.

3. Sew the red D strip to the left side and the red E strip to the bottom of the unit.

4. Sew the red F strip to the right side and the red G strip to the top of the unit.

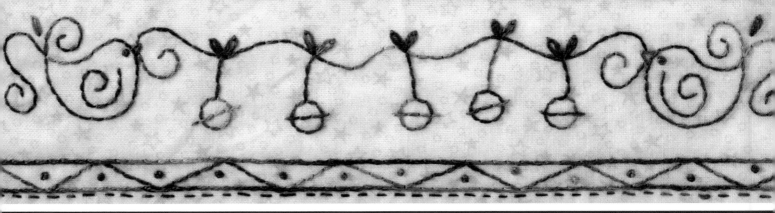

**5.** Sew the red H strip to the left side to complete the pillow front.

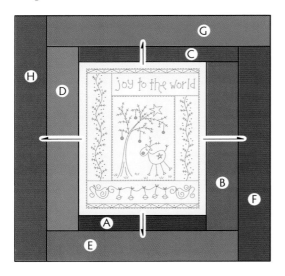

## Finishing the Pillow

**1.** Using a ¼" seam allowance and keeping right sides together, sew the two backing rectangles together along one long edge, leaving a 10"-wide opening in the center of the seam for turning and inserting the pillow insert. Press the seam allowances to one side.

**2.** Baste the pillow front to the batting square. Using pearl cotton and big-stitch quilting (see page 78), quilt ¼" from the seams in the red strips. Trim the batting even with the pillow top.

**3.** Aligning the raw edges and keeping *wrong* sides together, pin the pillow top to the pieced backing. Sew ¼" from the raw edges all the way around, pivoting at the corners.

**4.** Using the red 2½"-wide strips, make and attach the binding. Insert the 16" pillow form and stitch the opening closed.

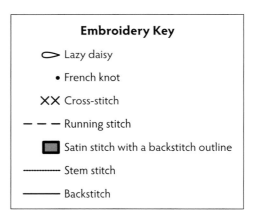

**Embroidery Key**

⌒ Lazy daisy

• French knot

✕✕ Cross-stitch

– – – Running stitch

◻ Satin stitch with a backstitch outline

·········· Stem stitch

——— Backstitch

**Joy to the World Pillow**

# HAPPY ELF BAG

*A friendly little elf decorates a mini Christmas sack.*

*Happy Elf Bag*

• FINISHED SIZE: 10" x 14" •

## Materials

*Yardage is based on 42"-wide fabric.*

⅜ yard of red floral for outer bag

⅜ yard of beige solid for lining

¼ yard of green floral for outer bag

1 rectangle, 7" x 9", of cream print for embroidery background

2 rectangles, 12" x 17", of batting

1 rectangle, 7" x 9", of lightweight fusible interfacing for embroidery backing

1½ yards of ⅛"-diameter cream cord

6-strand embroidery floss in variegated red/brown

Ecru pearl cotton, size 8

¼" quilter's tape (optional, see page 78)

Appliqué basting glue

## Cutting

**From the red floral, cut:**

1 strip, 10½" x 42"; crosscut into:

    2 rectangles, 3½" x 8½"

    1 rectangle, 3½" x 10½"

    1 rectangle, 10½" x 11½"

    2 squares, 3" x 3"

**From the green floral, cut:**

1 strip, 4½" x 42"; crosscut into:

    2 rectangles, 4½" x 10½"

    2 strips, 1½" x 8½"

**From the beige solid, cut:**

2 rectangles, 10½" x 15½"

## Embroidering the Designs

1. Using the pattern on page 28, trace the Elf design onto the right side of the cream rectangle. Fuse the interfacing rectangle to the wrong side of the marked rectangle.

2. Using two strands of floss, embroider the design, following the embroidery key on the pattern.

## Making the Bag Front and Back

1. Centering the embroidery, trim the stitched rectangle to 4½" x 8½".

2. Sew red 3½" x 8½" rectangles to opposite sides of the embroidered piece. Sew the red 3½" x 10½" rectangle to the top of the unit. Press all seam allowances toward the red rectangles.

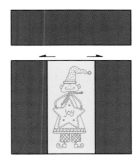 

**3.** Fold a red square in half diagonally, wrong sides together. Fold the square diagonally again, to make a prairie point. Repeat to make a second prairie point.

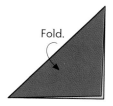

**4.** Pin the prairie points to the bottom of the embroidered rectangle, aligning the raw edges and slightly overlapping the points. Sew a green 4½" x 10½" rectangle to the bottom of the unit to make the bag front. Press the seam allowances as indicated.

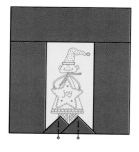

**5.** Sew the red 10½" x 11½" rectangle and the remaining green 4½" x 10½" rectangle together along their 10½" edges to make the bag back. Press the seam allowances toward the green rectangle.

## Quilting the Bag Front and Back

**1.** Baste the bag front to one of the batting pieces. Using pearl cotton and big-stitch quilting (see page 78), quilt ¼" from the seamline of the embroidered piece and ¼" from each side of the bottom seamline. Trim the batting even with the fabrics.

**2.** Baste the bag back to the remaining piece of batting and quilt ¼" from each side of the seamline. Trim the batting even with the fabrics.

## Assembling the Bag

**1.** To make a casing: On the wrong side of a green 1½" x 8½" strip, draw lines ½" from each long edge. On each side of the strip, fold the long edge over to meet the line and press well to make a ¼" hem. With the long edges pressed under, fold under ¼" on each end and press. Repeat to make the second casing.

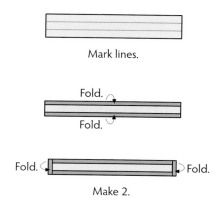

Mark lines.

Fold.
Fold.

Fold. Fold.

Make 2.

> **EASY CASING**
>
> *Use a little appliqué glue to hold the folded ends in place after pressing.*

2. Position one casing on the bag front, 1" from the top raw edge and an equal distance from each side. Using matching thread and backstitching at each end to secure, topstitch each long edge of the casing in place, leaving the ends open. Repeat for the bag back.

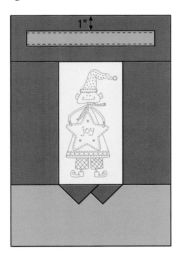

3. Pin the bag front and back, right sides together. Using a ¼" seam allowance, sew down one side of the bag, across the bottom, and up the other side. With the bag still wrong side out, box one bottom corner by bringing the bottom seam together with a side seam. Press flat and pin. Measure 2" from the corner and draw a line

perpendicular to the seams. Sew along this line and then trim ¼" from the stitching line. Repeat for the other corner.

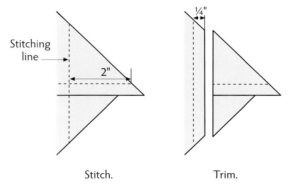

Stitching line

2"

¼"

Stitch. Trim.

4. Pin the beige rectangles right sides together. Using a ¼" seam allowance, sew down one long edge, across the bottom, and up the other long side, leaving a 3" opening for turning in the bottom seam. Leave the top open. Box the corners of the lining as you did for the bag. Do not turn the lining right side out.

5. Place the outer bag inside the lining, right sides together, matching the side seams. Pin along the top raw edge. Sew around the top edge. Turn the bag right side out through the opening in the lining. Slip-stitch the opening closed. Push the lining into the bag, smooth it out, and then press. Edgestitch ⅛" from the top edge.

## Finishing the Bag

Cut the cord in half to make two equal lengths. Thread one of the lengths through one casing and around through the other. Tie the cord ends in a knot. Repeat for the remaining length, starting at the opposite side of the bag. Pull the cords to close the bag.

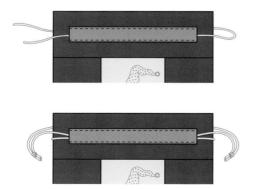

**Happy Elf Bag**

# REDBIRD CANDLE MAT

*Brighten the holidays with a redwork candle mat stitched with whimsical robins.*

*Redbird Candle Mat*

• FINISHED SIZE: 11" diameter •

## Materials

*Yardage is based on 42"-wide fabric.*

1 square, 14" x 14", of light-green check for
    embroidery background
1 strip, 1½" x 42", of red print for binding
1 square, 14" x 14", of fabric for backing
1 square, 14" x 14", of batting
1 square, 14" x 14", of lightweight fusible interfacing
    for embroidery backing
6-strand embroidery floss in variegated red

## Embroidering the Designs

1. Using the pattern on page 31, trace the Redbird
   design onto the right side of the light-green
   square. Make sure you trace the outer line of the
   hexagon, as this is your cutting line. Trace the
   design two more times to complete the hexagon
   shape as shown in the illustration above right.
   Fuse the interfacing to the wrong side of the
   marked square.

2. Using two strands of floss, embroider the designs,
   following the embroidery key on the pattern.

### SINGLE-FOLD BINDING

*For smaller projects such as this one, a wide,
double-fold binding is too bulky, so I use a
single-fold binding instead.*

## Finishing the Candle Mat

1. Layer the embroidered piece, batting, and
   backing; baste.

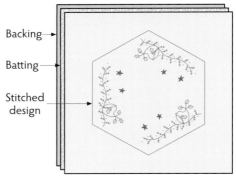

Backing

Batting

Stitched
design

Baste.

2. Using a single-fold binding, sew the red strip to
   the hexagon, aligning the raw edge of the strip
   with the hexagon outline. Trim all three layers
   even with the raw edge of the binding. Finish the
   binding by folding it over to the back and slip-
   stitching in place.

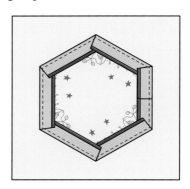

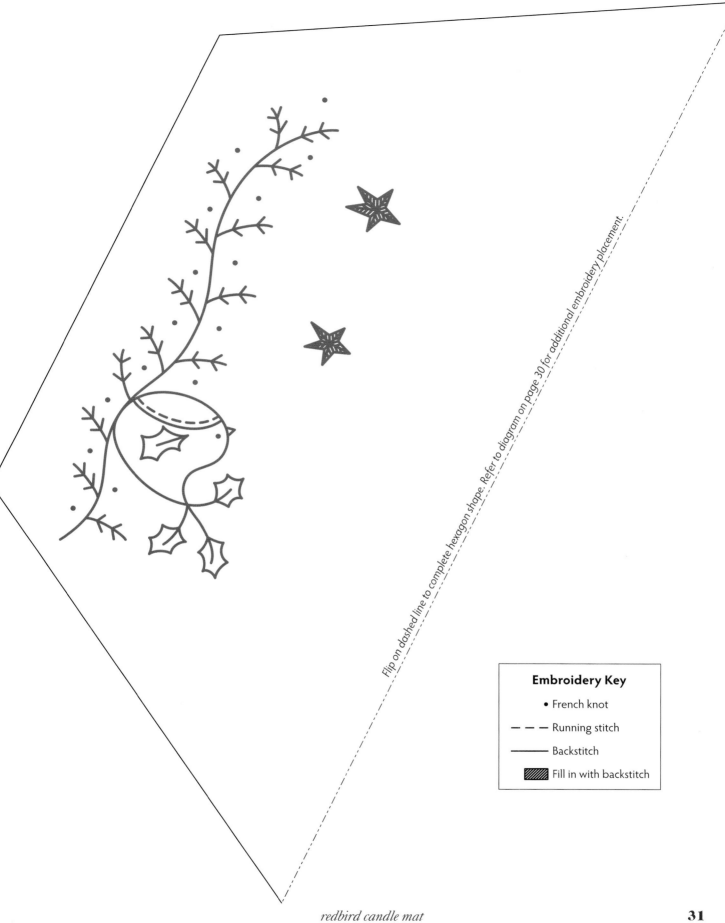

Flip on dashed line to complete hexagon shape. Refer to diagram on page 30 for additional embroidery placement.

**Embroidery Key**

- French knot

- - - Running stitch

——— Backstitch

▨ Fill in with backstitch

*redbird candle mat*

# HANGING FABRIC TAGS

*Create three sweet decorations for the tree, or to give as a gift!*

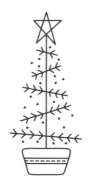

*Hanging Fabric Tags*

• FINISHED SIZE: 3" x 5½" •

## Materials

1 rectangle, *each* 4" x 6", of 3 different cream prints for embroidery background

1 rectangle, *each* 5" x 8", of 2 different red prints for piecing and backing of Tree and Child Is Born tags

1 rectangle, 5" x 8", of green print for piecing and backing of Bird tag

3 rectangles, 5" x 8", of lightweight batting

3 rectangles, 4" x 6", of lightweight fusible interfacing for embroidery backing

6-strand embroidery floss in red, dark green, brown, and yellow

Ecru pearl cotton, size 8

## Cutting

**From *each* of the green and red prints, cut:**

1 rectangle, 1½" x 4"

1 rectangle, 4" x 6"

---

### BATTING

*Using a lightweight batting makes it easier to turn the tags right side out.*

## Embroidering the Designs

1. Using the patterns on page 35, trace the tag outline onto the *wrong* side of each cream rectangle. Trace an embroidery pattern onto the right side of each cream rectangle, lining up the outer line. Fuse each interfacing rectangle to the wrong side of a marked rectangle.

2. Using two strands of floss, stitch the designs, following the embroidery key and color guides on the patterns.

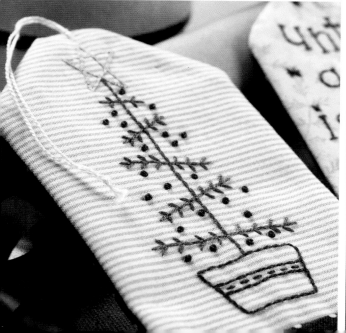

## Making the Tags

1. Trim the bottom of each stitched rectangle ¼" beyond the marked line.

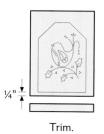

¼"

Trim.

2. Sew a green or red 1½" x 4" rectangle to the bottom of a stitched rectangle to make a tag front. Press the seam allowances toward the red or green rectangle.

3. With right sides together, align the raw edges of a tag front and a matching green or red 4" x 6" rectangle. Place the aligned pieces on a piece of batting and pin in place. Sewing on the marked tag line, stitch up one side, across the top, and down the other side. Do not sew the bottom edge. Turn right side out and press. Turn the bottom seam under ¼". Trim the batting from the seam allowance. Slip-stitch the bottom seam to close. Repeat to make a total of three tags.

4. Cut a 9" length of pearl cotton; thread a needle with a double strand. From the back of the tag, insert the needle through the top. Insert the needle through the loop formed by the thread. Pull tight and knot the ends of the thread.

**Embroidery Key**

◯ Lazy daisy

• French knot

✕✕ Cross-stitch

– – – Running stitch

—— Backstitch

**Hanging Fabric Tags**

# STAR BIRDS TABLE RUNNER

*Christmas birds adorn this festive table runner.*

*Star Birds Table Runner*

• FINISHED SIZE: 36½" x 16½" •

## Materials

*Yardage is based on 42"-wide fabric.*

½ yard of red print for Star block, sashing, and binding

⅓ yard of green print for Star block and outer border

1 fat quarter (18" x 21") of cream print for embroidery background

¼ yard of red-and-green floral for Star block and inner border

⅝ yard of fabric for backing

18" x 38" piece of batting

⅝ yard of lightweight fusible interfacing, 18" to 20" wide, for embroidery backing

Pearl cotton, size 12, in dark red, green, brown, and gold

Ecru pearl cotton, size 8

¼" quilter's tape (optional, see page 78)

## Cutting

**From the cream print, cut:**

1 strip, 11" x 21"; crosscut into 2 rectangles, 10" x 11"

**From the lightweight fusible interfacing, cut:**

2 rectangles, 10" x 11"

**From the red print, cut:**

1 strip, 3" x 42"; crosscut into:
    1 square, 2½" x 2½"
    4 strips, 1½" x 8½"
    8 squares, 1½" x 1½"

2 strips, 1½" x 42"; crosscut into 2 strips, 1½" x 30½"

3 strips, 2½" x 42"

**From the red-and-green floral, cut:**

1 strip, 2½" x 42"; crosscut into 8 squares, 2½" x 2½"

3 strips, 1½" x 42"; crosscut into:
    2 strips, 1½" x 10½"
    2 strips, 1½" x 32½"

**From the green print, cut:**

1 strip, 1½" x 42"; crosscut into:
    2 strips, 1½" x 6½"
    2 strips, 1½" x 8½"

3 strips, 2½" x 42"; crosscut into:
    2 strips, 2½" x 16½"
    2 strips, 2½" x 32½"

### FABRIC SELECTION

*You don't need to use Christmas-themed fabrics. Any red, green, and cream prints will work well for this project. I used reproduction prints for my table runner.*

## Embroidering the Designs

1. Using the pattern on page 40, trace the Star Birds design onto the right side of each cream rectangle. Fuse an interfacing rectangle to the wrong side of each marked rectangle.

2. Using one strand of pearl cotton, stitch the designs, following the embroidery key and color guides on the pattern.

## Making the Star Block

1. Draw a diagonal line on the wrong side of each red 1½" square. Aligning the corners, place a marked square on one corner of a red-and-green square. Sew directly on the marked line. Trim ¼" outside the seamline and press the seam allowances toward the red triangle. In the same way, sew a marked square on an adjacent corner to make a star-point unit. Make four units.

Make 4.

2. Lay out the star-point units, remaining red-and-green squares, and the red 2½" square in three rows as shown. Sew the pieces into rows. Press the seam allowances as indicated. Sew the rows and press the seam allowances toward the center.

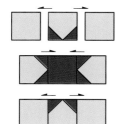 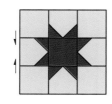

3. Sew green 1½" x 6½" strips to opposite sides of the star unit and press the seam allowances toward the green strips. Sew green 1½" x 8½" strips to the top and bottom of the unit to make a block. Press the seam allowances toward the green strips.

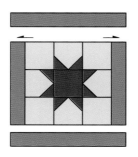 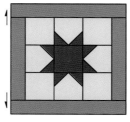

Make 1.

## Assembling the Table Runner

1. Centering the embroidered design, trim the stitched rectangles to 8½" x 9½".

2. Lay out the stitched rectangles, Star block, and red 1½" x 8½" strips as shown. Sew the pieces together to make a 30½"-long row. Press the seam allowances toward the red strips.

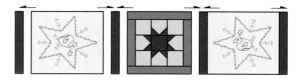

3. Sew red 1½" x 30½" strips to opposite sides of the row from step 2. Press the seam allowances toward the red strips.

4. Sew red-and-green 10½"-long strips to the ends of the row. Sew red-and-green 32½"-long strips to opposite sides of the table-runner center to complete the inner border. Press all seam allowances toward the red-and-green strips.

5. Sew green 32½"-long strips to opposite sides of the table-runner center. Then sew green 16½"-long strips to the ends of the table runner to complete the outer border. Press all seam allowances toward the green strips.

## Finishing the Table Runner

1. Layer the quilt top, batting, and backing; baste. Using ecru pearl cotton and big-stitch quilting (see page 78), quilt ¼" from the seamline in the green strips; quilt a wavy line in the center of the red strips.

2. Trim the batting and backing to the same size as the top.

3. Using the red 2½"-wide strips, make and attach the binding *before* completing the quilting next to the binding seam.

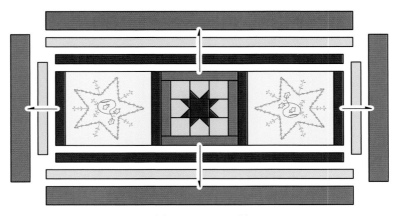

Table-runner assembly

*star birds table runner*

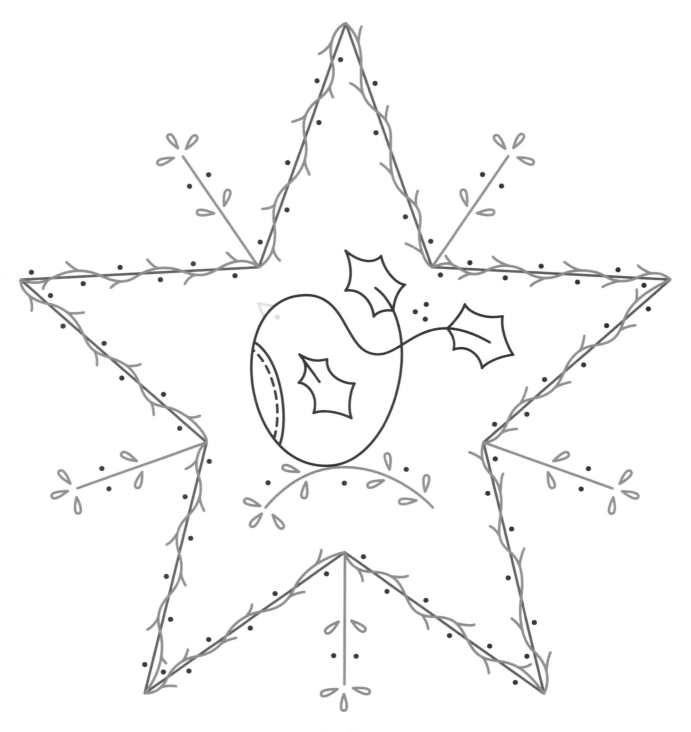

**Star Birds Table Runner**

**Embroidery Key**

◠ Lazy daisy

• French knot

– – – Running stitch

—— Backstitch

*christmas patchwork loves embroidery*

# SENTIMENTS MINI PILLOWS

*Embroider two adorable pillows with Christmas sentiments.*

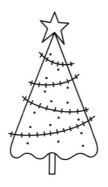

*Sentiments Mini Pillows*

• FINISHED SIZE: 7½" x 5½" •

## Materials

¼ yard *each* of a red and a green print for backing and binding

2 rectangles, 6" x 8", of cream print for embroidery background

2 rectangles, 6" x 8", of lightweight fusible interfacing for embroidery backing

5 decorative Christmas pins (optional)*

Pearl cotton, size 12, in red, green, yellow, and brown

Fiberfill for stuffing

*I used Just Pins–Holiday Assortment from Just Another Button Company. The pins are available at www.JustAnotherButtonCompany.com.*

## Cutting

**From *each* of the red and green prints, cut:**
2 rectangles, 4¼" x 5½"
1 strip, 1½" x 30"

## Embroidering the Designs

1. Using the patterns on page 43, trace each Sentiments design onto the right side of a cream rectangle. Fuse each interfacing rectangle to the wrong side of a marked rectangle.

2. Using one strand of pearl cotton, stitch the designs, following the embroidery key and color guides on the patterns.

## Making the Mini Pillows

Make one or both—they're quick little stocking stuffers!

### Tree Pillow

1. Centering the embroidery, trim the stitched Tree rectangle to 5½" x 7½".

2. Using a ¼" seam allowance and with right sides together, sew the two green rectangles along one long edge to make the backing, leaving a 1½"-wide opening for turning. Press the seam allowances to one side.

3. Aligning the raw edges, and with *wrong* sides together, pin the stitched rectangle to the pieced backing. Machine baste ⅛" from the raw edges.

4. Using a single-fold binding and the green strip, bind the pillow. Fold the binding over to the back and slip-stitch in place.

5. Stuff firmly with fiberfill. Hand stitch the opening closed.

### Bird Pillow

Make as for the Tree pillow, using the red rectangles and red strip. Decorate the pillow with Christmas pins, as desired.

hearts come home for christmas

**Embroidery Key**

◡ Lazy daisy

• French knot

✕✕ Cross-stitch

— Backstitch

wish upon a Christmas tree

**Sentiments Mini Pillows**

# A MERRY LITTLE CHRISTMAS WALL HANGING

*Enjoy a wall hanging wishing you a merry Christmas.*

*A Merry Little Christmas Wall Hanging*

• FINISHED SIZE: 12½" x 13½" •

---

## Materials

*Yardage is based on 42"-wide fabric.*

1 fat eighth (9" x 21") of red print for border

1 rectangle, 9" x 10", of cream print for embroidery background

¼ yard of green stripe for binding

1 rectangle, 14" x 15", of fabric for backing

1 rectangle, 14" x 15", of batting

1 rectangle, 9" x 10", of lightweight fusible interfacing for embroidery backing

60" length of ⅜"-wide cream rickrack

6-strand embroidery floss in red, dark red, light green, medium green, dark green, brown, and yellow

Ecru pearl cotton, size 8

¼" quilter's tape (optional, see page 78)

Pigma pen

Appliqué basting glue

## Cutting

**From the red print, cut:**

1 strip, 2½" x 21"; crosscut into 2 strips, 2½" x 9½"

2 strips, 2½" x 12½"

**From the green stripe, cut:**

2 strips, 2½" x 42"

## Embroidering the Designs

**1.** Using the pattern on page 47, trace the Merry Little Christmas design onto the right side of the cream rectangle. Fuse the interfacing rectangle to the wrong side of the marked rectangle.

**2.** Using two strands of floss, stitch the designs, following the embroidery key and color guides on the pattern.

## Assembling the Wall-Hanging Top

**1.** Centering the embroidery, trim the stitched rectangle to 8½" x 9½". Sew the red 2½" x 9½" strips to the sides of the stitched rectangle. Press the seam allowances toward the red strips. Sew the red 2½" x 12½" strips to the top and bottom of the rectangle. Press the seam allowances toward the red strips.

2. Measuring 1" from the seamlines and using a Pigma pen, draw lines all around the center rectangle as shown. Glue baste the rickrack on top of the lines, trimming when needed. Hand stitch the rickrack in place.

## Finishing the Wall Hanging

1. Layer the wall-hanging top, batting, and backing; baste. Using pearl cotton and big-stitch quilting (see page 78), quilt ¼" inside the center rectangle.

2. Trim the batting and backing to the same size as the top.

3. To make an optional hanging sleeve prior to binding, fold the ends of a 4" x 11" strip under ¼" twice and topstitch to hem. Fold the strip in half lengthwise, *wrong* sides together, and press. Aligning the raw edges, stitch the folded strip to the top of the wall-hanging back, ⅛" from the raw edges.

4. Using the green 2½"-wide strips, make and attach the binding. Stitch the lower (folded) edge of the sleeve to the backing by hand.

**Embroidery Key**

- Lazy daisy
- French knot
- ✕✕ Cross-stitch
- – – – Running stitch
- —— Backstitch
- ▨ Fill in with backstitch

**A Merry Little Christmas Wall Hanging**

# CHRISTMAS STOCKINGS

*Christmas Stockings*

• FINISHED SIZE: 8" x 15" •

## Materials

*Yardage is based on 42"-wide fabric.*

½ yard *each* of green and red prints for stocking bodies

⅝ yard of cream print for stocking lining

1 square, 4" x 4" *each*, of 6 assorted red and 6 assorted green prints for stocking cuffs

2 rectangles, 5" x 8", of cream prints for embroidery background

4 rectangles, 10" x 16", of batting

2 rectangles, 5" x 8", of lightweight fusible interfacing for embroidery backing

12" length of ⅜"-wide white rickrack for hanging loops

6-strand embroidery floss in red and variegated green

Ecru pearl cotton, size 8

¼" quilter's tape (optional, see page 78)

Template plastic

Appliqué basting glue

## Cutting

**From *each* of the assorted red prints, cut:**
2 rectangles, 1½" x 3½" (12 total)

**From *each* of the assorted green prints, cut:**
2 rectangles, 1½" x 3½" (12 total)

## Embroidering the Designs

1. Using the patterns on page 54, trace the oval design onto the right side of each cream rectangle; these are your appliqué lines. Trace the embroidery designs onto the ovals. Fuse the interfacing rectangles to the wrong side of each marked rectangle.

2. Using two strands of floss, embroider the designs, following the embroidery key and color guides on the pattern.

## Making the Stocking Front and Back

Instructions are for making the green stocking. Repeat the steps to make the red stocking.

1. Cut out the embroidered oval ¼" beyond the marked appliqué line to create a ¼" turn-under allowance.

2. Trace the stocking pattern on pages 52 and 53 onto template plastic, making sure to join the pieces as indicated on the pattern. Cut out the template. On the right side of the green print, trace around the template to make a stocking, then flip the template over to trace a reversed stocking. Cut out the stocking on the drawn line.

3. With the design upright, position the stitched oval on the right side of a stocking piece (toe pointing to the left), so the appliqué line is 1" from the top raw edge and the oval is centered

between the sides. Glue baste it in place by applying several pinhead-sized dots of appliqué glue about an inch apart near the middle of the oval. Using needle-turn appliqué (see page 78), stitch the oval in place, turning the edge under just until the appliqué line is no longer visible.

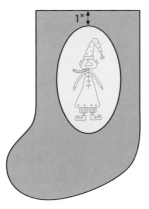

**4.** Join six red 1½" x 3½" rectangles along their long edges to make a 3½" x 6½" cuff. Press the seam allowances in one direction. Repeat to make a second red cuff.

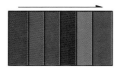

Make 2.

**5.** Sew a red cuff to the top of each green stocking piece. Press the seam allowances toward the stocking.

## Quilting the Stocking Front and Back

**1.** Baste the stocking front to one of the batting rectangles. Using pearl cotton and big-stitch quilting (see page 78), quilt ¼" beyond the appliquéd oval and ¼" from each side of the seamlines in the cuff. Trim the batting even with the fabrics.

**2.** Baste the reversed stocking (stocking back) to the remaining piece of batting and quilt ¼" from each side of the seamlines in the cuff. Trim the batting even with the fabrics.

## Assembling the Stocking

**1.** Pin the stocking front and back right sides together. Using a ¼" seam allowance and starting at the cuff, sew down one side of the stocking, around the toe, and up the other side. Turn the stocking right side out. On the cuff only, quilt ¼" from each side of each side seam.

**2.** Cut a 6" length of rickrack and fold it in half to make a hanging loop. On the back of the stocking (next to the seam that comes from the heel), place the loop on the outside the stocking, with the loop hanging down and the raw edges even with the top of the cuff. Pin in place.

**3.** Use the stocking template to trace one stocking and one reversed stocking onto the lining, making sure to add 3" to the top of each stocking. Cut out the stocking lining pieces.

**4.** Pin a stocking lining piece and reversed lining piece right sides together. Using a ¼" seam allowance and starting at the top, sew down one side of the stocking, around the toe, and up the other side, leaving a 3" opening along the heel edge as shown.

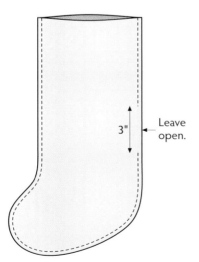

**5.** Place the outer stocking inside the lining, right sides together, matching the side seams. Pin in place, and then sew around the top raw edges. Turn the stocking right side out through the opening at the heel. Sew the opening in the lining closed. Push the lining inside the stocking and press well. Topstitch around the upper edge of the stocking, ⅛" from the edge.

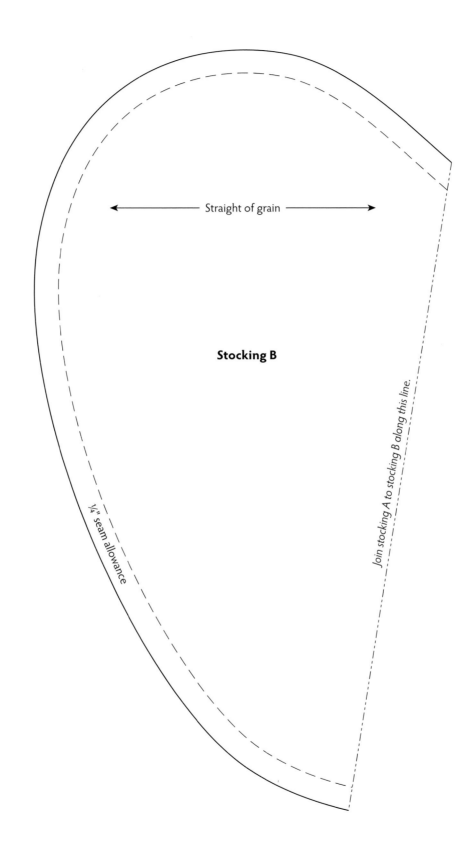

Straight of grain

**Stocking B**

Join stocking A to stocking B along this line.

¼" seam allowance

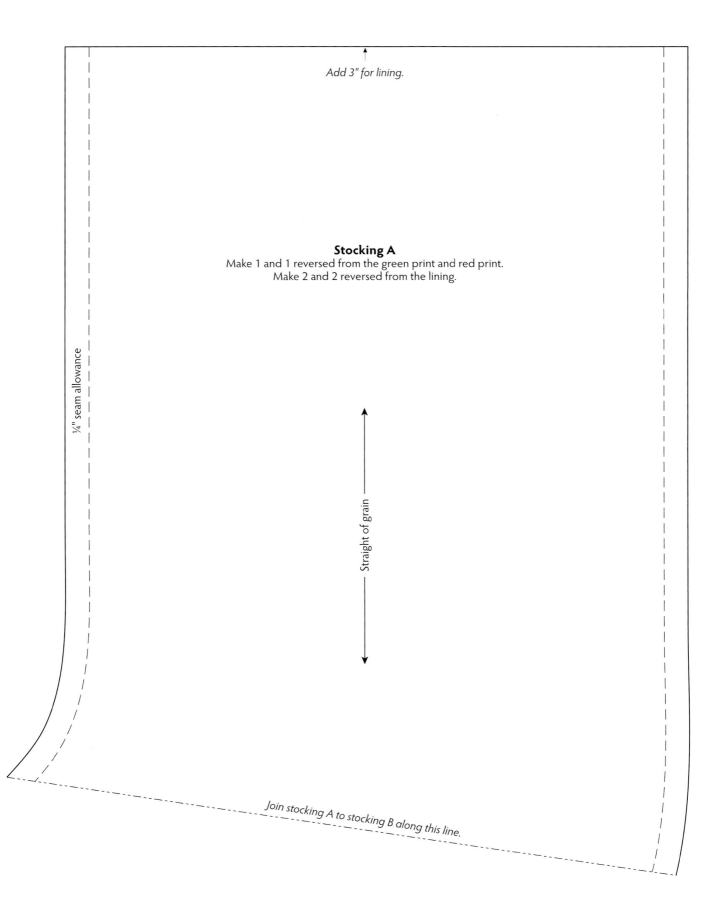

Add 3" for lining.

**Stocking A**
Make 1 and 1 reversed from the green print and red print.
Make 2 and 2 reversed from the lining.

¼" seam allowance

Straight of grain

Join stocking A to stocking B along this line.

## Embroidery Key

◯ Lazy daisy

• French knot

XX Cross-stitch

– – – Running stitch

——— Backstitch

**Christmas Stockings**

# TREE SKIRT

*Try hexagons for a different take on the traditional tree skirt.*

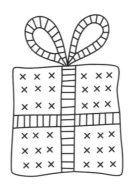

*Tree Skirt*

• FINISHED SIZE: 34" x 37½" •

## Materials

*Yardage is based on 42"-wide fabric.*

1⅛ yards *each* of red print, green dot, and red-and-green floral for hexagons and backing

½ yard of cream solid for embroidery background

40" x 40" piece of batting

¾ yard of lightweight fusible interfacing, 18" to 20" wide, for embroidery backing

6-strand embroidery floss in red, green, and yellow

Ecru pearl cotton, size 8

¼" quilter's tape (optional, see page 78)

Template plastic

Appliqué basting glue

4 hook-and-eye closures, size 2

## Cutting

**From the cream solid, cut:**

2 strips, 6" x 42"; crosscut into 12 squares, 6" x 6"

**From the lightweight fusible interfacing, cut:**

12 squares, 6" x 6"

## Embroidering the Designs

1. Using the patterns on pages 59–61, trace different Word designs onto the right side of six cream squares. Using the patterns on page 62, trace the Present and Star designs, three times each, onto the right side of the remaining cream squares. Trace the hexagon outline also; it forms your appliqué lines. Fuse a square of interfacing to the back of each square.

2. Using two strands of floss, stitch the designs, following the embroidery key and color guides on the patterns.

## Making the Hexagons

1. Trace the hexagon on page 63 onto template plastic and cut out. Using the hexagon template, cut out six red, six green, and six red-and-green floral hexagons. Use the same template to cut 18 hexagons from the batting.

2. Trace the hexagon pattern onto another piece of template plastic, then draw a second line 1" from the first line. Cut out to make a backing template. Use the backing template to cut out six red, six green, and six red-and-green floral hexagons.

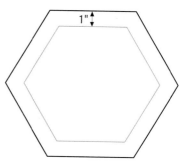

3. Center an embroidered Word hexagon on the right side of a small red hexagon. Glue baste it in place by applying two pinhead-sized dots of appliqué glue, about 1" apart, near the middle of the hexagon. Using needle-turn appliqué (see page 78), stitch the embroidered hexagon in place, turning the edge under just until the appliqué line is no longer visible. Repeat to appliqué a Word hexagon on each small red hexagon. Using two strands of yellow floss, freehand embroider a running stitch inside each appliquéd hexagon (not marked on the design). Appliqué the Present and Star embroidered hexagons onto each of the small red-and-green floral hexagons. Using two strands of green floss, freehand embroider a running stitch inside each Present hexagon. Using two strands of red floss, freehand embroider a running stitch inside each Star hexagon.

4. Layer an appliquéd red hexagon, batting hexagon, and green backing hexagon; baste. Using pearl cotton and big-stitch quilting (see page 78), quilt ¼" from the appliquéd hexagon.

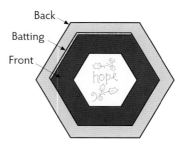

5. To make a binding, fold the edges of the green hexagon to meet the edges of the red hexagon; press. Then, fold the green hexagon again, placing the folded edge on top of the red hexagon, covering the raw edges. Slip-stitch along the folded edge, carefully folding the corners into 60° angles.

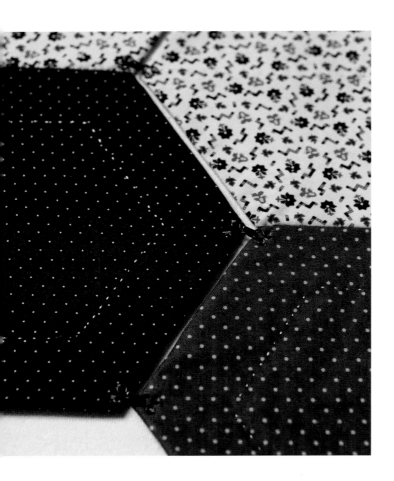

6. Repeat steps 4 and 5 using the appliquéd red-and-green floral hexagons and red backing hexagons.

7. Layer the green hexagons, batting, and red-and-green floral backing hexagon; baste. Using pearl cotton and big-stitch quilting, quilt three lines across each green hexagon from point to point as shown in the photo on page 55. Repeat step 5 to bind each hexagon.

## Assembling the Tree Skirt

1. Lay out the hexagons in a circular formation, with the green hexagons in the middle. Place the appliquéd hexagons around the green ones, alternating the Word hexagons with the Present and Star hexagons. Note there is not a hexagon in the center of the tree skirt.

2. Slip-stitch the hexagons together, leaving an opening between a Word and a Present hexagon and their accompanying green hexagons as shown in the assembly diagram below.

3. Sew a hook-and-eye closure on the corners of each hexagon along the opening. Use the hook-and-eye closures to secure the tree skirt around the base of your tree.

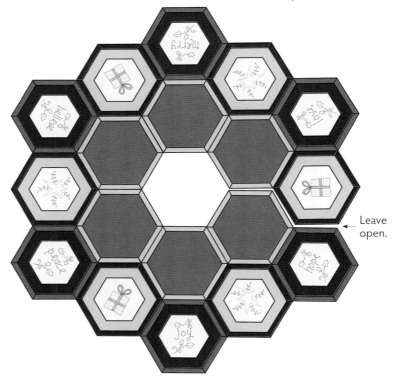

Leave open.

Tree Skirt assembly

*christmas patchwork loves embroidery*

**Embroidery Key**

- • French knot
- —— Backstitch

**Tree Skirt**

**Embroidery Key**

- • French knot
- ✕✕ Cross-stitch
- —— Backstitch

**Tree Skirt**

**Embroidery Key**

- French knot
- ✗✗ Cross-stitch
- ──── Backstitch

**Tree Skirt**

**Embroidery Key**

◯ Lazy Daisy

✕✕ Cross-stitch

- - - Running stitch

—— Backstitch

**Tree Skirt**

*christmas patchwork loves embroidery*

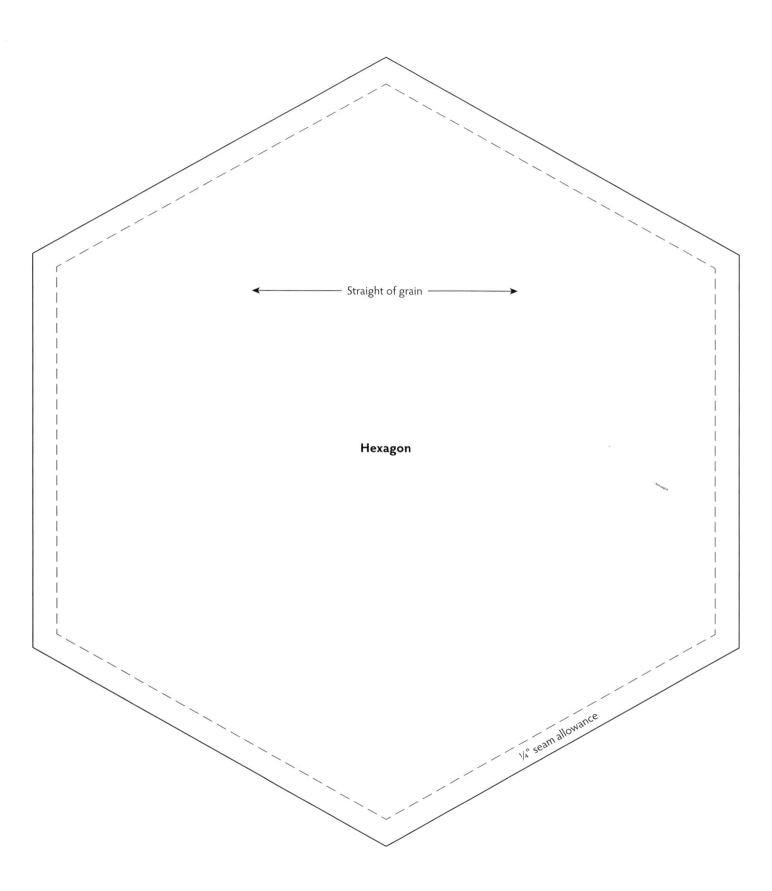

Straight of grain

**Hexagon**

¼" seam allowance

# HEART AND HOME WALL HANGING

*Decorate your home with this whimsical wall hanging.*

keep Christmas in
your heart ♡♡ and
home, all year long

*Heart and Home Wall Hanging*

• FINISHED SIZE: 23½" x 24½" •

## Materials

*Yardage is based on 42"-wide fabric.*

⅜ yard of red star print for border

⅓ yard *total* of assorted prints for squares and rectangles

1 fat quarter (18" x 21") of cream fabric for embroidered blocks

⅓ yard of green print for binding

¾ yard of fabric for backing

26" x 27" piece of batting

⅝ yard of lightweight fusible interfacing, 18" to 20" wide, for embroidery backing

6-strand embroidery floss in red

## Cutting

**From the cream fabric, cut:**

1 rectangle, 8" x 10"

1 rectangle, 5" x 9"

1 square, 4" x 4"

1 rectangle, 4" x 7"

**From the lightweight fusible interfacing, cut:**

1 rectangle, 8" x 10"

1 rectangle, 5" x 9"

1 square, 4" x 4"

1 rectangle, 4" x 7"

**From the assorted prints, cut a *total* of:**

27 squares, 2½" x 2½"

11 rectangles, 2½" x 3½"

2 rectangles, 1½" x 3½"

1 rectangle, 1½" x 4½"

**From the red star print, cut:**

3 strips, 3½" x 42"; crosscut into:

 2 strips, 3½" x 18½"

 2 strips, 3½" x 23½"

**From the green print, cut:**

3 strips, 2½" x 42"

## Embroidering the Designs

1. Using the patterns on pages 69 and 70, trace the House design onto the right side of the cream 8" x 10" rectangle. Trace the Tree design onto the right side of the cream 5" x 9" rectangle. Trace the Heart design onto the right side of the cream 4" square. Trace the Saying design onto the right side of the cream 4" x 7" rectangle. Fuse the interfacing rectangles and square to the wrong side of each marked rectangle and square.

2. Using two strands of floss, embroider the designs, following the embroidery key on the pattern.

## Assembling the Wall Hanging

1. Centering the embroidered designs, trim the House block to 7½" x 9½", the Tree block to 4½" x 8½", the Heart block to 3½" x 3½", and the Saying block to 3½" x 6½".

2. Sew a print 1½" x 3½" rectangle to the left of the Saying block. Join two print 2½" squares and a print 2½" x 3½" rectangle to make a strip. Sew the strip to the top of the Saying block. Sew the House block to the top of the pieced strip. Press the seam allowances as indicated.

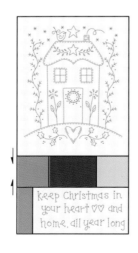

3. Sew a print 1½" x 3½" rectangle to the right of the Heart block; then sew a print 1½" x 4½" rectangle to the top of the Heart block. Join two print 2½" squares and sew them to the bottom of the Heart block. Sew the Tree block to the bottom of the two-square strip. Press the seam allowances as indicated.

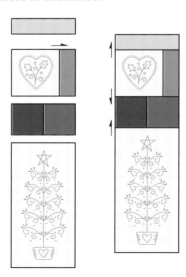

*christmas patchwork loves embroidery*

**4.** Sew together four print 2½" squares and two print 2½" x 3½" rectangles to make a strip. Press the seam allowances as indicated.

**5.** Lay out the sections from steps 2 and 3; place the strip from step 4 between the sections. Join the sections and center strip. Press the seam allowances toward the center.

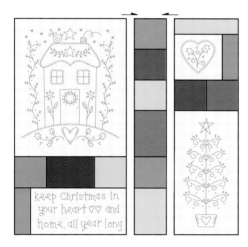

## Adding the Borders

Refer to the wall-hanging assembly diagram on page 68 as needed throughout. Press all seam allowances toward the just-added border.

**1.** Join five print 2½" squares and one print 2½" x 3½" rectangle to make the top border. Sew the border to the top of the center block.

**2.** Join five print 2½" squares and two print 2½" x 3½" rectangles to make the left side border. Sew the border to the left side of the center block.

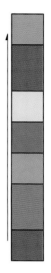

**3.** Join two print 2½" x 3½" rectangles and five print 2½" squares to make the right side border. Sew the border to the right side of the center block.

**4.** Join three print 2½" x 3½" rectangles and four print 2½" squares to make the bottom border. Sew the border to the bottom of the block.

**5.** Sew a red star-print 18½"-long strip to each side of the wall-hanging top. Sew red star-print 23½"-long strips to the top and bottom of the wall hanging.

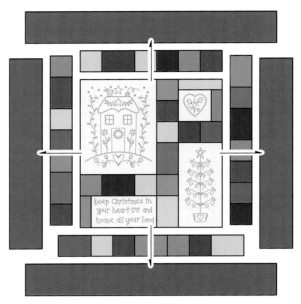

Wall-hanging assembly

## Finishing the Wall Hanging

**1.** Layer the wall-hanging top, batting, and backing; baste. Quilt as desired. The wall hanging on page 64 was machine quilted using a meandering design of stars, hearts, and holly leaves. A holly design was quilted in the border.

**2.** Trim the batting and backing to the same size as the top.

**3.** To make an optional hanging sleeve prior to binding, fold the ends of a 5" x 30" strip under ¼" twice and topstitch to hem. Fold the strip in half lengthwise, *wrong* sides together, and press. Aligning the raw edges, stitch the folded strip to the top of the quilt back, ⅛" from the raw edges.

**4.** Using the green 2½"-wide strips, make and attach the binding. Stitch the lower (folded) edge of the sleeve to the backing by hand.

**Embroidery Key**

◠ Lazy daisy

• French knot

– – – Running stitch

—— Backstitch

**Heart and Home**

Keep Christmas in
your heart ♥ and
home, all year long

**Heart and Home**

# COMFORT AND JOY CARD FOLDER

*Keep holiday cards and your wish lists in this festive folder.*

*Comfort and Joy Card Folder*

• FINISHED SIZE: 9½" x 12½" •

## Materials

*Yardage is based on 42"-wide fabric.*

⅝ yard of red print for pockets and binding

⅜ yard of green print for front, pockets, and back

1 fat quarter (18" x 21") of cream floral for lining

1 rectangle, 7" x 9", of beige print for embroidery background

1 rectangle, 13" x 27", of batting

2 rectangles, 7½" x 12½", of batting

1 rectangle, 7" x 9", of lightweight fusible interfacing for embroidery backing

40" length of ¼"-wide red rickrack

22" length of ¼"-wide cream ribbon

6-strand embroidery floss in variegated red/green

Ecru pearl cotton, size 8

## Cutting

**Following the diagram at right and cutting in the order listed below, cut from the green print:**

1 strip, 1½" x 42"; crosscut into 2 strips, 1½" x 12½"

1 rectangle, 9½" x 12½"

1 rectangle, 7½" x 12½"

1 rectangle, 7½" x 8½"

1 strip, 3" x 9½"

1 strip, 2" x 9½"

2 strips, 2" x 8½"

**Following the diagram at right, cut from the red print:**

2 strips, 2½" x 42"

1 strip, 12½" x 42"; crosscut into:
    4 rectangles, 7½" x 12½"
    1 rectangle, 7½" x 8½"

**From the cream floral, cut:**

1 rectangle, 12½" x 18½"

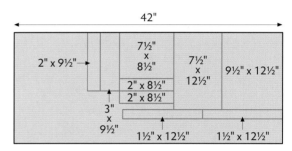

Cutting diagram for green print

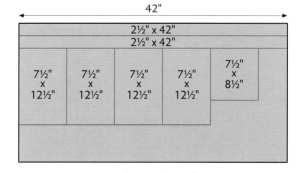

Cutting diagram for red print

## Embroidering the Designs

1. Using the pattern on page 75, trace the Comfort and Joy design onto the right side of the beige rectangle using your preferred method. Fuse the interfacing rectangle to the wrong side of the marked rectangle.

2. Using two strands of floss, embroider the designs, following the embroidery key on the pattern.

## Making the Folder Cover

1. Centering the embroidery, trim the stitched rectangle to 6½" x 8½".

2. Sew the green 2" x 8½" strips to the sides of the trimmed rectangle. Press the seam allowances toward the strips. Sew the green 2" x 9½" strip to the top of the rectangle and the green 3" x 9½" strip to the bottom of the rectangle to make the folder front. Press the seam allowances toward the green strips.

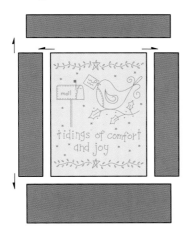

3. Sew the green 9½" x 12½" rectangle to the left side of the folder front. Press the seam allowances as indicated.

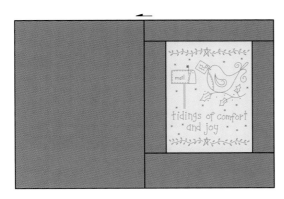

4. Draw a line 1½" from the bottom edge. Sew a 19" length of rickrack on top of the marked line.

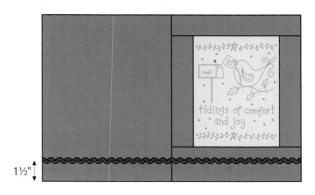

1½"

5. Layer the cover and the 13" x 27" batting rectangle; baste. Using pearl cotton and big-stitch quilting (see page 78), quilt wavy lines above and below the rickrack, and quilt a wavy line in the center of the side and top borders on the front. Trim the batting even with the fabric.

## Making the Folder Pockets

1. To make a large folder pocket, place a 7½" x 12½" batting rectangle between two red 7½" x 12½" rectangles, *wrong* sides together. Repeat to make a second large folder pocket.

2. For the remaining pockets, fold the green 7½" x 12½" rectangle in half, wrong sides together, to form a 7½" x 6¼" rectangle. Press and then topstitch along the folded edge. Sew a 7½" length of rickrack along the fold. Fold the green 7½" x 8½" rectangle in half, wrong sides together, to form a 7½" x 4¼" rectangle. Press and then topstitch along the folded edge. Sew a 7½" length of rickrack along the fold. Fold the red 7½" x 8½" rectangle in half, wrong sides together, to form a 7½" x 4¼" rectangle. Press and then topstitch along the folded edge.

3. Place the red 7½" x 4¼" pocket on the green 7½" x 6¼" pocket, with side and bottom edges aligned. Mark a line 2" from the right side and stitch along this line to form a small pocket for a pen. Place the layered pockets on a large red pocket from step 1, with side and bottom edges aligned. Pin in place. Use a green 1½" x 12½" strip to bind the right edge.

4. Place the green 7½" x 4¼" pocket on the remaining large red pocket, with side and bottom edges aligned. Pin in place. Use a green 1½" x 12½" strip to bind the left edge.

5. Place each pocket section on the cream rectangle, with the binding edges facing toward the center. Pin and then baste the pockets in place, ⅛" from the raw edges.

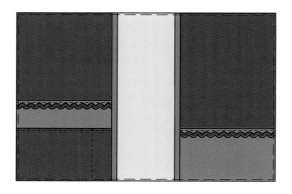

## Assembling the Folder

1. Place the quilted cover on top of the pocketed lining, *wrong* sides together. Pin generously to hold both sections together. Sew a vertical line through the center of the folder. Cut the cream ribbon in half to make two ties. Place a tie on each side of the quilted cover, centered between the top and bottom edges, and with the cut ends and raw edges aligned. Pin in place.

2. Using the red 2½"-wide strips, make and attach the binding to the top and bottom edges.

**Heart and Home**

**Embroidery Key**

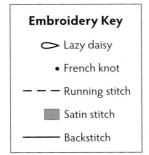

Lazy daisy

• French knot

- - - Running stitch

Satin stitch

—— Backstitch

# GENERAL INSTRUCTIONS

The projects in this book combine hand embroidery with piecing and hand quilting. In this section, I'll review some of the basic embroidery information you'll need, but if you're new to sewing and quilting, you can find additional helpful information for free at ShopMartingale.com/HowtoQuilt, where you can download illustrated how-to guides on everything from rotary cutting to binding a quilt.

## Embroidery Instructions

Below are the tools and techniques I like best. But there are many embroidery techniques, so try as many ways as you can to find the stitches, threads, fabrics, and techniques that work for you.

### *Needles*

Hand-sewing needles come in packages labeled by type and size. The larger the needle size, the smaller the needle (a size 1 needle will be longer and thicker than a size 12 needle). For embroidery, I like to use a size 8 embroidery needle (also referred to as a crewel needle). An embroidery needle is similar to a Sharp, but with an elongated eye designed to accommodate six-strand floss or pearl cotton. You may prefer a size 7 or 9. For appliqué, I use a size 10 straw needle (also called a milliner's or appliqué needle), but a size 9 or 11 may be your preference. When hand quilting with size 8 pearl cotton, I prefer to use a size 5 or 6 embroidery needle. This allows me to thread the needle easily. Test a few needles until you find one that suits you; any brand is fine.

### *Threads*

I like to use a variety of threads. Some threads I select to match the fabrics I plan to use; sometimes I pick a thread first, and then choose appropriate fabrics. Six-strand embroidery floss is the most common floss used. It needs to be split before stitching, since only two or three strands are used at once. I used two strands for most of the projects in this book.

Some threads, such as the pearl cotton I use when quilting, can be used straight off the spool or ball. I always knot my threads when embroidering. Because the embroidered squares are backed with fusible interfacing before being stitched, you don't need to worry that the knots are going to show through. To start embroidering, thread your needle with the appropriate floss and make a knot at the end of the strand. When you have about 4" to 5" of floss left, or when you're finished using a color, pull the needle to the back of the embroidery. Then, loop the thread around the needle and push the resulting knot close to the back of the stitch you've just finished.

My favorite threads for embroidery are Aurifil Mako Cotton 12-weight thread; 6-strand embroidery floss from DMC, Cottage Garden Threads, and Weeks Dye Works; the Gentle Art sampler threads; and size 12 pearl cotton from DMC or Valdani. My favorite thread for quilting is DMC size 8 pearl cotton. I've used all of these threads in the projects in this book.

### *Tracing the Design*

To trace or transfer the embroidery design onto your fabric, I recommend using a light box. Tape the design in place on the light box, and then center the fabric on top of the design and secure it in place. Use a brown fine-point Pigma pen to trace lightly over the design. A fine-point washable marker, a ceramic pencil (such as Sewline), or a mechanical or wooden pencil with a fine, hard lead will also work.

If you don't have a light box, tape the design to a window or use a glass-topped table with a lamp underneath. I always trace the minimum. For instance, if you're tracing lazy daisy stitches (loops on the embroidery pattern), mark a dot only where you will start the stitch. Leave dotted lines (running stitches) untraced, stitching where they appear by referring to the illustration or photo. You'll soon find the sort of marking that works best for you.

### *Embroidery Fabric and Interfacing*

For easier tracing, choose a light-colored fabric for the background. It's OK to use a subtle print, such as a small polka dot; the print will add some interest. Tone-on-tone fabrics are also nice to use.

I always back my traced fabric with a very lightweight fusible interfacing. This prevents show-through of the embroidery threads and knots. And, because the interfacing stiffens the fabric a bit, there is less distortion of the fabric and stitches when the embroidered piece is hooped. To do as I do, cut a piece of interfacing the same size and shape as your background fabric and, following the manufacturer's instructions, fuse it in place *after* you've traced the design and *before* you start stitching.

## Hoops

I use an embroidery hoop to keep the fabric taut, but not tight, while stitching. Hoops are available in wood, metal, and plastic, with different mechanisms for keeping the fabric taut. Any type of hoop is fine, so take the time to find one you're comfortable with. A 4" hoop is my preferred size, but you may prefer a 5" or 6" hoop. Remember to always remove your fabric from the hoop when you've finished stitching for the day.

# Sewing and Quilting Instructions

Please read through the instructions carefully before starting. For all projects, the yardage is based on 42"-wide fabric, the seam allowances are always ¼", and I usually press the seam allowances away from the embroidered fabric and toward the darker fabrics.

## Appliqué

For some projects in this book I've embroidered the design onto the background fabric first, and then used needle-turn appliqué to stitch it in place on the appropriate item. If you wish to do likewise, trace the appliqué line onto the background fabric when tracing the design. Once you've finished the stitching, cut out the embroidered design, leaving a scant ¼" seam allowance from the appliqué line.

On inner curves, clip into the seam allowance up to, but not through, the marked line. Avoiding the edges, baste the embroidery in position with appliqué glue. Roxanne Glue-Baste-It is my favorite appliqué glue because it enables me to place tiny, controlled dots of glue exactly where I want them, and it's also 100% water soluble. Working a half inch at a time, use the tip of the needle to turn under the seam

allowance along the marked line, and secure it in place using thread that matches the appliqué fabric and very small slip stitches or blind stitches.

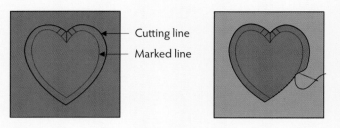

Cutting line
Marked line

## Batting

I like to use cotton batting in all my quilts. For smaller projects, such as "Hanging Fabric Tags" (page 32) or "Sentiments Mini Pillows" (page 41), a lightweight batting is preferable. Fiberfill is used in the mini pillows.

## Quilting

To add a little dimension to my projects, I use big-stitch quilting and size 8 ecru pearl cotton to hand quilt my projects. I begin by placing ¼" quilter's tape so that one side adjoins a seamline or other feature of my project, such as an embroidered circle. Stitching along the other edge of the tape allows me to stitch a quilting line that is even and exactly ¼" from the seam. Quilter's tape comes on a roll and is both inexpensive and repositionable.

Thread your needle with the end straight off the ball, and cut the thread to about 15" long. Knot one end with a single knot. Insert your needle through the backing fabric to the front, where you want to start. Pull the backing fabric away from the batting and pull on the thread. Tug gently so the knot pops into the layers. Bring the needle up through the quilt top right next to your ¼" quilter's tape, and then insert it back into the quilt right next to the ¼" tape and approximately ¼" from the spot where your needle came up. This will make a big stitch approximately ¼" long. Bring the needle back up next to the tape and ¼" from the point where the needle went down last. Continue in this manner until your thread is approximately 4" to 5" long. Take the thread to the back, knot the thread, and then pull the knot back into the quilt, between the backing and the batting, bringing the needle out approximately 1" away. Trim the thread close to the backing fabric.

# EMBROIDERY STITCHES

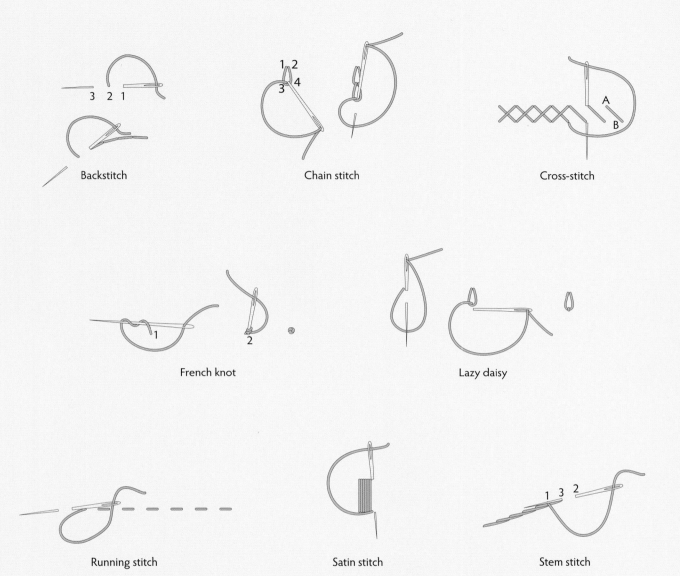

Backstitch

Chain stitch

Cross-stitch

French knot

Lazy daisy

Running stitch

Satin stitch

Stem stitch

# MEET THE AUTHOR

*My name is Gail Pan,* and I live on the outskirts of Melbourne, Australia, at the foot of the beautiful Dandenong Ranges (a series of low, verdant mountain ranges). Growing up in a home where sewing was always an important part of life, it was only natural that I tried every craft there was! I have always had some kind of project in the works, trying everything from knitting to cross-stitch.

When my kids were little I made their clothes, and when they got too old for that, I moved on to patchwork. My design business was born out of my habit of always adapting whatever I'm working on until it becomes a new design altogether. In 2003, at the encouragement of some friends who were opening their own patchwork business, I began to design and release my own patterns. I have been designing ever since!

I teach all over the world and get great satisfaction and enjoyment from sharing my love of needle and thread. I have also met some amazing women whom I now call friends. Happy stitching!